Pilgrimage

PRODUCED BY KINNARA

Sarnath, India 3

Photographs by Alan Ohashi and Dean Koga

Designed by Qris Yamashita

Heian International Publishing Co.
P.O. Box 2402
South San Francisco, CA 94080

ISBN 0-89346-011-7

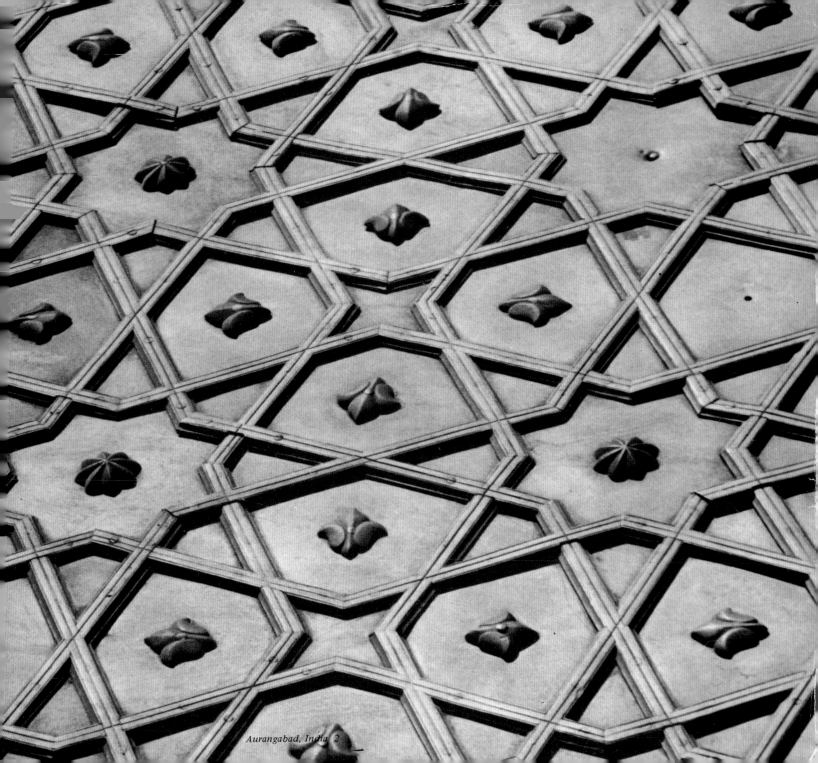

Aurangabad, India 2

The Buddha has often been called "The Greatest Son of Mother India." Certainly his impact upon Asia, and in recent times his impact on the world, has been great. His teachings have profoundly influenced Asian civilizations for the past 2500 years. Yet Buddhism was not to remain in the land of its birth. The Dharma was carried to all of Asia, and in recent years to Europe and the Americas, but it was to disappear in India itself. Depending upon how one wishes to look upon it, Buddhism was rejected or absorbed by the land of its birth. The number of Buddhists in India today number a few million at most. The great monasteries, universities, hospitals, etc. which once flourished have long since fallen into ruin. The sacred sites of Buddhist India are today miniscule fragments of their former glory.

Yet the sacred sites remain, maintained by the Indian government and supported by Buddhists the world over. In this century, Buddhists have moved to re-establish their ancient connections with the Buddhist homeland. Restoration of temples and monasteries has begun; institutions of Buddhist study have been established; and new monasteries and pilgrimage hostels have been built. International gatherings of Buddhists have brought about a greater awareness of the diversity of Buddhist traditions and helped to clarify what we share in common. The Buddhist homeland has been the catalyzing agent in this process.

Technically, there are almost no Buddhists in India and the Buddhist sites are largely ruins from a golden past. Yet our pilgrimage to India was not simply a visit to a museum of dead things. India, if nothing else, is religious. Religion is still a serious pursuit. The religious quest is not a separate quest in India. It is not separate from the agonies and ecstatic moments of everyday life. It permeates the fabric of Indian life from its costliest silks to its coarsest homespun. The incense of religion is sometimes delicate and refined, sometimes offensive, sometimes reeking of corruption. It is full of traps and cages, abuses and fanaticism. But it is more often than not pursued with a natural goodness we found disarming to our jaded sophistication. Like one's relations with one's own parents, we were frustrated with, appalled by, delighted with, inspired by, and profoundly moved by our encounter with religion in India. It is with a sense of deep gratitude that we dedicate this book to "Bharata Ma"—to Mother India.

—Kinnara Pilgrimage Group—

Agra, India 4

From November 23rd, 1974, through January 8th, 1975, 23 Americans made a pilgrimage to the Buddhist sites of Nepal, India and Sri Lanka. The pilgrimage was sponsored by Kinnara, a Buddhist study group made up of members from various Buddhist schools but primarily from the Jodoshinshu school. The members of the pilgrimage ranged in age from 20 to 50 years old, including four priests of the Jodoshinshu school. Baggage was limited to one backpack and travel and living accomodations were largely 2nd and 3rd class. This enabled the group to make the trip for approximately $1400 per person, which included all room, board, and transportation. With two or three exceptions, room was at Indian-style hotels and Buddhist hostels.

Other than Omairi (religious services) at the Buddhist sites, there were no planned activities. Each pilgrim was left to discover and explore on his or her own. The group met each morning and each evening for sitting and chanting meditation.

The photographic account of the pilgrimage is followed by a short section containing information of travel, food, lodging and sites of interest. The photographs were taken by two members of the pilgrimage; Alan Ohashi and Dean Koga. Layout was by Qris Yamashita and Alan Ohashi. Text was by Masao Kodani and running commentary by pilgrimage members and Masao Kodani.

Rajgir, India 5

Bodhgaya, India 6

The Sacred Sites of Buddhism

The sites in India held to be sacred by
Buddhists the world over are found largely in
the northern state of Uttar Pradesh and the
northeastern state of Bihar. The state of Bihar
is the homeland of Buddhist India. The name of
the state is derived from the word "Vihara" or
Buddhist monastery. Such "Vihara" were once
found scattered throughout the area. Bihar
today is one of the poorest states in India, a
sharp contrast to its early history as a center of
wealth, prosperity and culture. The terrain is
flat and stony with only an occasional low rise
of soft mountains.

There are three seasons in Bihar, as is generally the case throughout India. Winter is the
season from October through March. It is by far
the most comfortable time of the year, much like a
California springtime. Summer is from late
March through May. Summer in Bihar can be
severe with temperatures well over 100 degrees
Fahrenheit and strong, dry winds. The land dries
and cracks under the intense heat and all activity
seems to come to a halt. Everything waits for the
all-important rains. The Monsoon normally
comes in June and lasts until September. It is a
season of intermittent rains which make the land
blush a brilliant green almost overnight. One is
made deeply aware of the crucial importance of
the rains.

It is in this land that Siddhartha Gautama
lived for 80 years, seeking, discovering, and
spreading the Truth of life-and-death. From the
time of his Enlightenment some 2,500 years ago,
this land has been venerated by Buddhists throughout Asia as the homeland of the Buddha, the
"Awakened One." Until his death at the age of

eighty, the Buddha spent the last 45 years of his life spreading his teaching of Wisdom-Compassion, constantly moving from one city or village to the other. Out of the many extraordinary events in the life of this extraordinary man, Buddhist tradition has pinpointed four principal events and their locations. These four locations are considered the most imporant sites of Buddhist pilgrimage.

The Four Pilgrimage Sites
Lumbini Garden
Lumbini is the site of the birth of the Buddha. The Buddha was born Siddhartha Gautama, son of King Shuddhodana and Queen Maya of the ruling family of the clan known as the Shakya. Gautama was the family name and the Buddha is variously referred to as the Buddha Shakya-muni (Sage of the Shakya Clan). Gautama Buddha, the Prince Siddhartha (his given name) etc. The land of the Shakya was located in what is today the southern part of the Kingdom of Nepal. Its capital was at Kapilavastu. It was the custom of that time that a woman give birth to her children at the home of her parents. It was in accordance with this custom that Queen Maya left Kapilavastu for the home of her parents as the time for the birth of her child approached. It was while resting from her journey at the garden called Lumbini that the child was born. According to the Japanese Buddhist tradition, the Buddha-to-be was born Siddhartha Gautama on the 8th day of April, 563 B.C., in Lumbini Garden.

Prince Siddhartha grew up in princely luxury in the city of Kapilavastu, eventually marrying the Princess Yashodara and having a son, Rahula.

Bodhgaya, India 7

Kathmandu, Nepal 8

Bodhgaya, India 9

He led a life of comparative ease and comfort, all the while experiencing a growing need to solve the riddles of life's sufferings. At the age of 29, Siddhartha resolved to seek the way to spiritual liberation from the ills of the world. Leaving his wife and son, he wandered for 6 years studying under eminent religious teachers and diligently applying himself to ascetic practices.

The site of Lumbini today is called Rummindei and is located in Nepal a few miles from the Indian border state of Uttar Pradesh. Little remains of the many monasteries and temples said to have flourished there. The most important of the remains is a highly polished pillar of stone commemorating the visit of the Emperor Ashoka in the 3rd century B.C. and which authenticates the site of Lumbini.

Buddha-Gaya

The site of the Great Enlightenment. In the 6th year of his quest for enlightenment, Siddhartha rejected the practices of asceticism. He sat in meditation under a fig tree and resolved not to move from it until enlightenment was his. On the morning of the 8th day of the 12th month (according to Japanese Buddhist tradition), Siddhartha became the Buddha, the "Awakened One." The tree under which he sat has come to be known as the Bodhi Tree, the Tree of Enlightenment. The descendant of this tree (Ficus Religiosa) still grows at the spot of Siddhartha's Enlightenment, in the shadow of the Mahabodhi Temple (the Temple of the Great Enlightenment) which rises 170 feet to mark the center of the Buddhist world.

Buddha-Gaya, or Buddh-Gaya, or Bodh-Gaya today is a quiet little village 8 miles to the south of the city of Gaya in the Gaya District of Bihar State. The Mahabodhi Temple with its soaring tower dominates the entire area. The Bodhi Tree exerts an attraction which is difficult to describe yet easy to feel. The area is made up of two tiny villages interspersed with temples and monasteries of virtually every Buddhist country in the world. This is the most important of the four major sites and Buddhist pilgrims from all over the world flock to it. Here in Buddha-Gaya the goal of all Buddhists was first attained—the goal of enlightenment.

Buddha-Gaya is a microcosm of the world. The sacred and the profane do not live side-by-side but as one organic whole: monks performing day-long obeisances in front of the Bodhis tree; hawkers selling strings of beads, pressed Bodhi Tree leaves, old coins, and newly made "antiques;" villagers planting or harvesting their crops; pilgrims performing Puja (religious services) in Vietnamese, Hindi, Chinese, Japanese, Singhalese, Tibetan, Thai, Nepali, and English; children playing in open fields; housewives and merchants bargaining with flails for hands; tour guides with flags and megaphones; etc., etc., etc. It is a shock to ones preconceptions of a "holy place"; it is a delight to the mind's eye; it is an overwhelming carnival of seriousness and frivolity, of profound wisdom and shallowness, of gentle understanding and granite ignorance. And over it all stands the tower of the Mahabodhi Temple and an ancient tree with pointed leaves—it is another planet, yet there is a deep sense of having returned to something familiar.

Bodhgaya, India 10

Nalanda, India 11

Sarnath

Lumbini was the physical birthplace of Prince Siddhartha. The spiritual birthplace of Prince Siddhartha was at Buddha-Gaya. At Buddha-Gaya the Prince Siddhartha became the Buddha Shakyamuni. From Buddha-Gaya the new-born Buddha traveled to Sarnath, a place of quiet to the north of the city of Benares. In Sarnath, at the site called Deer Park, the Buddha preached his first sermon to five men who had earlier practiced asceticism with him. This was the first teaching of the content of his enlightenment and is referred to as the First Turning of the Wheel of the Dharma.

Sarnath is some 6 miles to the north of the city of Benares or Varanasi as it is called today. It is in the state of Uttar Pradesh. The Deer Park at Sarnath today consists of monastery ruins and stupas (dome-shaped reliquary structures) covering an area of several acres. The monastery complex is largely from the 4th century A.D., at which time it housed some 1500 monks. A commemorative pillar erected by the Emperor Ashoka is located near the main shrine of the complex. The lion capital of this pillar, which is housed in the nearby Sarnath Museum, has been adopted as the state emblem of India. The museum houses an outstanding collection of Buddhist art and artifacts, attesting to the immense creativity of Buddhism in India.

Sarnath is the beginning of the 2500 year history of Buddhist missionary work. For over

1000 years of India's long history, monks and laymen followed the footsteps of the Buddha, establishing monasteries, hostels, hospitals, and great universities. The Deer Park at Sarnath represents this beginning.

Kushinara

For the next 45 years, until his death at the age of 80, the Buddha wandered from village to village spreading his teachings and gaining an increasing number of monk and lay followers. He accepted men and women into his order without regard to caste rules. His wife and son also entered the order. During the time of the heavy rains, the Buddha would stop at retreat sites donated by wealthy lay followers, there to concentrate on instructing the monks. These sites have become the secondary sites of pilgrimage.

After a long life of missionary work, the Buddha died in a small village called Kushinara. The site today is known as Kushinagara, a still small village in the northernmost part of the state of Uttar Pradesh. Lying on his right side with his head to the north, the Buddha passed into Nirvana after admonishing his disciples to "Be lamps unto yourselves. Seek salvation alone in the Truth. Rely upon yourselves and do not rely upon external help." The Buddha's body was cremated and his ashes divided among his followers. At Kushinagara today, a small temple housing the recumbent figure of the Buddha marks the place of his death. Nearby is the ruin of a stupa the size of a small mountain which marks the place of cremation. The site is surrounded by the foundations of monasteries long vanished but still overseen by a few resident monks from other Buddhist countries.

Sanchi, India 12

Ellora Caves, India 13

Bodhgaya, India 14

Secondary Buddhist Pilgrimage Sites
Rajagriha

Rajagriha or Rajgir, as it is called today, was once the capital of the powerful Maghada Kingdom which flourished during the time of the Buddha. The name Rajagriha means "royal palace." The city is in the Patna District of Bihar State and is famous for its association with the Buddha and Mahavira, the last of the Jaina Tirthankaras. The city is surrounded by five mountains which are heavily wooded. Sections of the massive city wall which once stretched some 30 miles in circumference can still be seen.

The Buddha frequently visited Rajagriha and was highly regarded by the ruling King Bimbisara and later, by Bimbisara's son King Ajatashatru. Many of the Buddha's sermons are recorded to have been given in this famous city, in the Bamboo Grove Vihara donated by a layman, and in the Mango Grove Vihara donated by the court physician Jivaka. Overlooking the city is the Saptaparni Cave where the first Buddhist Council of 500 disciples of the Buddha was held, 6 months after his death. On another peak is the Vishwa Shanti Stupa, built in 1970 in dedication to the principle of world peace. This was accomplished through the efforts of Rev. Nittatsu Fujii, a Japanese Buddhist priest who has dedicated his life to building such stupas throughout the world. The stupa in Rajagriha is the 22nd in the series.

Nalanda

The ruins of Nalanda University lie a few miles to the north of the city of Rajagriha. The immense ruins that can be seen are only a portion of what is known to still lie buried beneath

Varanasi, India 15

the earth. From the 6th to the 13th century A.D., Nalanda was the great seat of learning in Asia. Students from Central Asia, China, Tibet, and Southeast Asia came to study at this great Buddhist university under the most renown scholars of the ancient world. At its peak over 10,000 monks and students were in residence in what amounted to a university city. Nalanda was also noted for its beautiful buildings of five and six stories and numerous towers, all delicately painted and decorated with carvings and shining roof tiles. The curriculum not only included all branches of Buddhism, but also Vedic studies, general literature, philosophy, logic, grammar, medicine, metal casting, rhetoric, etc. Among Nalanda's list of renown scholars are Nagarjuna, Silabhadra, Arya Deva, Vasubandhu, Dignaga, Dharmakirti, Atisa Dipankara, and Padma Sambhava. The vitality of Nalanda declined in the 13th century and the death blow was dealt to it by invading Muslims.

Sanchi

Though not associated with the life of the Buddha, Sanchi is world famous for its remarkably preserved Buddhist monuments and famous stupa. Beginning in the 3rd century B.C. and continuing into the 14th century A.D. Sanchi was a monastic community for approximately 1000 years. It is located in the state of Madhya Pradesh near the city of Bhopal. The Great Stupa at Sanchi is a masterpiece of early Buddhist art and one of the finest examples of the development of the stupa as a simple burial mound into the highly refined reliquary of the remains of the Buddha and Buddhist sages it is today. The stone gateways surrounding the stupa are intricately and sensitively carved to depict the many incidents in the life of the Buddha and in the lives of his former incarnations. Of the eight stupas built by the Emperor Ashoka here at Sanchi, three remain. Monks of the Mahabodhi Society maintain a temple and hostel in Sanchi for Buddhist pilgrims and visitors.

Ajanta & Ellora

The cave temples of Ajanta and Ellora lie some 20 miles and 65 miles respectively from the city of Aurangabad in Maharashtra State. Ajanta is a series of 29 Buddhist Chaitya and Vihara carved into the living rock of a cliff. These cave temples and monasteries were laboriously chiseled out of the side of a cliff over a period of 600 years from the 1st through the 6th centuries A.D. The inner walls of the buildings are covered with the earliest existing examples of Indian painting. Executed in vibrant colors and sensuous lines, the paintings depict the life of the Buddha and earthy scenes from everyday life; voluptuous court ladies, dancers, royal processions, merchants, etc. Buddhas, Bodhisattvas, flying gods and goddesses, fantastic animals, etc., etc., are painted or carved into the rock.

The Buddhist caves at Ellora date from the 7th century A.D. when, for reasons yet unknown, the Buddhists abandoned Ajanta. Ellora is a series of Jain, Hindu, and Buddhist cave and rock-cut temples, 12 of which are Buddhist. The Buddhist caves consist of Chaitya and Vihara carved into the cliff, one of them having 3 stories with galleries of carved Buddhas. Cave number 10 is a Chaitya with carved pillars and a large central Buddha image which is illuminated by a horseshoe-shaped window above the entrance to the cave.

New Delhi, India 16

We look up and wonder —
not so much of India's past nor of her future,
but of this incredible present.

Delhi, India 17

Delhi, India 18

These ancient buildings
are new in the history
of my people.

Delhi, India 19

Have you no eyes or heart
to appreciate our labors
for these many hundreds of years?

Khajuraho, India 22

Kandy, Sri Lanka 21

Rajgir, India 23

New Delhi, India 24

New Delhi, India 25

Like old family pictures – formal
and full of dignity.

New Delhi, India 26

Kathmandu, Nepal 28

Jalgaon, India 29

Tiruchirapalli, India 30

Aurangabad, India 31

Kathmandu, Nepal 32

Patan, Nepal 33

While weaving they sing.
How strange we must seem.
With our talk of business vs pleasure,
Work vs play, active vs retired life.
Dividing and compartmentalizing our
Lives, then putting them together
And saying, "We are now whole".

Patan, Nepal 34

Kathmandu, Nepal 35

Kathmandu, Nepal 37

What does it mean
to call this sacred and that profane,
this religious and that secular,
this feeling and that thought?

Kathmandu, Nepal 36

Bodhgaya, India 38

I am India: I give you milk, curds, ghee;
I pull your plow and cart; I give you
the dung to build your cooking fires
and to purify your hearths;
I clean your streets and carry your wares;
I give all that is asked of me —
I am India.

There was so much that happened to me before, during and after the Pilgrimage; but it seems like it would take forever to explain.

Let me say my reasons for going. I came to a point in my life when I asked myself, 'what's life all about?' I couldn't see myself working everyday, forty hours a week, behind a desk. What would I have accomplished 30 years from now? What would I have to show? Is this what life is all about?

It occurred to me that Reverend Mas was taking a group to India. I really thought the rest were crazy to want to go to India. It was out of convenience that I decided to go. If I hadn't been thinking about life, I probably would have never considered going on this pilgrimage.

My biggest hang-up during the trip was with my ego. I was afraid to talk to the native people, and I seemed to color everything the way I wanted it to be. In looking back, it seems like it was all a dream—seeing women working in the fields, eating at roadside stands, sleeping together on concrete floors, chanting at Bodhgaya, riding crowded busses and trains, walking the country roads, etc.

It was some experience visiting places where Shakyamuni Buddha had once been, to see temples, to see people other than Japanese paying respects to the Buddha and meditating and chanting, to see the Bodhi Tree, Sarnath, to talk to Ceylonese Buddhists. I was able to grasp a new insight into Buddhism. The Pilgrimage made Buddhism more real and meaningful to me.

Even though I haven't found the solution to why I am here on Earth, each day I came to understand myself and my life a little better.

Overall, the Pilgrimage was a fantastic experience. For sure, I would like to go back to India. This is one trip I will never forget.

—Norman

Agra, India 39

Of beautiful women
and their smiles,
Of lovely thoughts
and graceful wiles.

Agra, India 41

New Delhi, India 42

In youth and in old age, it is
a blessing to be in the company of children.
If to you this is a dubious blessing,
stop and consider —
what better thing is there for you to do?

Madras, India 43

Khajuraho, India 44

Before the beginning of things—
there was water, and light,
and music.

Rajgir, India 45

It is not the tea that nourishes and refreshes —
but the offering of it.

Khajuraho, India 46

Khajuraho, India 47

Bodhgaya, India 48

Feed me auntie! And give me a smile for dessert.
I do not want to again stray away
from things that matter.

Negombo, Sri Lanka 49

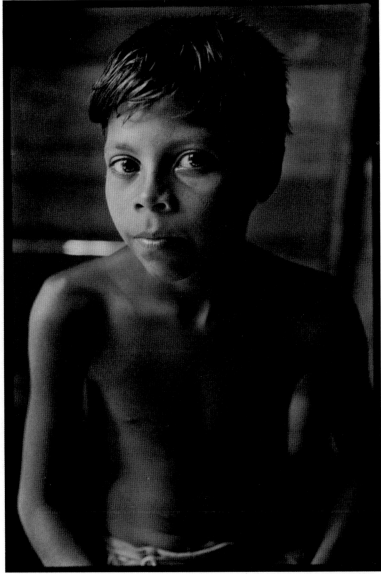

A scarlet thread,
A lump of brown cane sugar,
A pet lizard on a string,
And lights that dance in the eyes of children.

Negombo, Sri Lanka 50

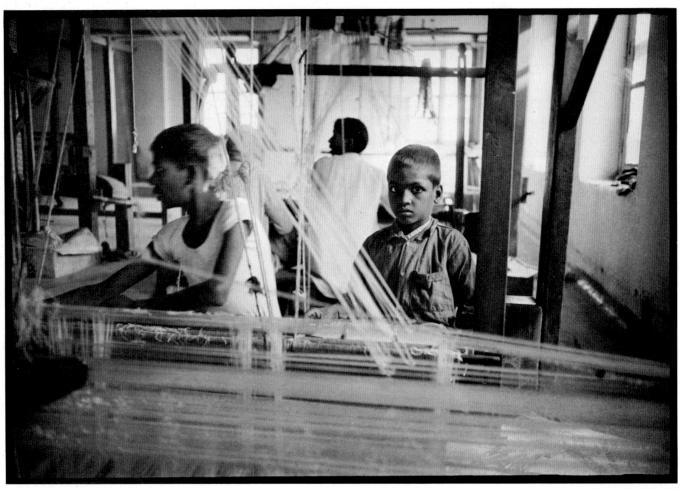

Varanasi, India 51

With eyes clear and deep,
Like white lotus blossoms
Waving over the dark water.

Bodhgaya, India 52

Things were so much bigger,
And brighter, and exciting
When I was a child.
Am I now more mature,
Or am I just — dying away?

Varanasi, India 53

And I will carry lights in procession on the day of your wedding.
Flames of vivid color will mark the day you wed.
We will dress up and come to watch in awe and happiness
at the union of a prince and princess.

Sanchi, India 55

The earth is not ours to use up as we see fit.
Neither is it ours to protect and defend.
We are a part of the Great Earth and not separate from it.
It is the twisted view that we are separate from the earth
that causes us to greedily destroy it or greedily protect it —
in either case, it is an arrogance which plugs our ears
to the song of the Great Earth.

New Delhi, India 56

Agra, India 57

What is it that moves so deeply within us
that we create with such loving care
memorials, testaments, monuments,
and rituals to death?
Is it a creative whim, a fear, a triumph of the spirit,
what is it?

Varanasi, India 58

Varanasi, India 59

Varanasi, India 60

At the Ganges one waits,
One absorbs the stillness
Of this supporter of life
And receiver of death.

Agra, India 61

As they looked at me,
we all smiled
knowing that we would not pass this way again.

Khajuraho, India 63

Aurangabad, India 64

Sarnath, India 65

O people of the world;
father and son, sister and brother, husband and wife,
families and relatives immediate and distant —
love and revere one another,
do not hate nor be jealous of one another,
be not covetous or begrudging,
be always benign in speech and manner,
and do not be devious with each other.

— from the Sukhavativyuha Sutra —

I bow in reverence to the ever-abiding Buddha.
I bow in reverence to the ever-abiding Dharma.
I bow in reverence to the ever-abiding Sangha.

Bodhgaya, India 66

Bodhgaya, India 67

And Siddhartha sat beneath a tree of
pointed, heart shaped leaves.
And in the third watch of the night,
the cloud of Ignorance was pierced.
From Siddhartha emerged the Buddha,
The Awakened One.

Bodhgaya, India 68

Travel Notes for Pilgrims

The travel information given here is for pilgrims who are neither excessively rich nor excessively poor. Though not sleeping under trees and bathing in rivers, it is to some extent roughing it. None of the accomodations listed here are what Americans would consider first class. For our group, luxurious accomodations meant hot water, private bathroom, and a printed menu. By and large, the accomodations listed required each of us to carry our own supply of soap, toothbrush, toothpaste, and toilet paper. Outside of the major cities, such toilet articles are unavailable, and even in the major cities are difficult to obtain and expensive.

Clothing

During the winter months in Nepal and northern India, a warm jacket or coat is necessary for the chilly evenings. Otherwise light cotton clothing or wash and wear is all that is necessary. In the warmer and more humid southern part of India and Sri Lanka, cotton clothing is especially recommended for its ability to 'breathe.' Sandals are the most comfortalbe and convenient footwear and are readily available at a wide range of prices.

Food
NEPAL

Unlike India, meat dishes are widely available in Kathmandu. With a large Tibetan population, Tibetan-Chinese style cooking is widely available. Noodles, beef, pork, goat, chicken, and a variety of vegetables make up a filling and inexpensive menu. The spicy curries and vegetarian dishes of the Nepali kitchen are equally good and inexpensive. There are many first-class hotels in Kathmandu with first-class restaurants at first-class prices. For even the slightly adventurous however, you can get a very good inexpensive meal in the local downtown restaurants. A full meal will cost anywhere from 50 cents to $1.50.

Be careful of the water! Your best bet is to drink tea (chai) or 'hot lemon' (boiled water with lemon and sugar) which is about 5 cents a glass or cup. As a general rule, avoid raw vegetables.

INDIA

The Buddhist sites in India are generally off the beaten tourist path, and meals are largely limited to food stall fare. Vegetarian meals are the general rule with some chicken dishes. The curried dishes range from spicy to searing hot but are well worth trying. For those who must have meat dishes, look for Muslim or Tibetan restaurants. The word "hotel" in the Indian countryside means "restaurant." These are simple meals of curried vegetables with rice or a variety of fry-bread. Outdoor stalls serve snacks for seven or eight cents. These include Puri, a dab or curried vegetable on a small circle of fry-bread; Pakora, vegetables coated in batter and deep fried; Paratha, piecrust-like tarts filled with vegetables; and in the south, Dosa, a water-thin bread made from lentil flour. Printed menus are non-existent but the proprietors are usually more than happy to spend the time deciphering your English and sign language requests. "Fancy" restaurant meals will cost 50 cents to $1.00. In the cities of New Delhi, Bombay, Madras, etc., you may want to splurge on a sumptuous meal costing from $3 to $5. Otherwise, one can get along quite well at the

New Delhi, India 69

"hotel" restaurants and outdoor stalls. There is also an endless variety of sweets, desserts, and seasonal bananas, oranges, mangoes and other fruits for a few pennies each. In the south, you can get a refreshing and safe drink of coconut water for 2 cents—the coconuts are opened when you purchase them. As a rule of thumb, purchase foods which have been cooked, drinks for which the water has been boiled, and fruits which have thick skins or can be peeled. In the north, "chai" or tea with milk and sugar is everywhere available. In the south, try some of the best coffee in the world.

SRI LANKA

Sri Lanka, formerly Ceylon, is a tropical country with an enormous variety of fruits and vegetables. Seasonal fruits include mangoes, mangosteens, grapefruit, oranges, guava, beli, pawpaw, custard apples, pears, and the evil-smelling but delicious durian. Sri Lanka curry dishes are some of the hottest anywhere so order carefully. Try string hoppers, a noodle dish made from rice; or hoppers, a kind of griddlecake with an egg baked on top of it. Ceylonese tea is world famous and deservedly so, as is their coffee. A full and filling meal will cost from $1.50 to $2.50. Many hotels and guest houses include two meals with their rooms. The breakfast is generally large and more than adequate until evening. An added treat is the availability of ice cream in the large towns and cities. Though prices are generally higher in Sri Lanka than in India or Nepal, there is a greater variety and quantity of food.

Lodging and Travel
NEPAL
Kathmandu

The capital of the Hindu Kingdom of Nepal, Kathmandu can be reached by daily flights from New Delhi, Varanasi (Benares), Patna, or Calcutta. If you have time, take the overland road from the Indian border town of Raxaul, Bihar State to Kathmandu by bus or jeep. It takes from 8 to 12 hours but is a breathtaking trip through the Nepali countryside and down into the Kathmandu valley. The group flew from New Delhi to Kathmandu and was rewarded with a view of the awesome Himalayan range. Upon landing at the airport, we were approached by a number of people from various hotels in the city. There is also a very helpful tourist information booth at the airport. After comparing prices, we decided on the Hotel Manaslu which is in the medium range of accomodations which are available in the city. Double rooms with bath (hot water sometimes) ran between $4.00 to $6.00 per room per day. The Manaslu was formerly the palace of a former prime minister. It is located immediately behind the New Royal Palace and is run by a young and enthusiastic staff of graduates from the College of Hotel Management. The restaurant on the ground floor has a large menu of Tibetan-Chinese dishes.

For Buddhists, two sites in Kathmandu are of some importance: SWAYAMBUNATH—A Tibetan temple said to have been visited by the Buddha. It stands upon a hillock overlooking the city. One can climb the many steps leading to the top or walk the gradually sloping road which winds around the hill to the rear of the temple complex. The stupa with its gilded tower has four pairs of eyes painted at the base of the tower—the all-seeing eyes of the Buddha looking in all directions. Within the main sanctuary and in the grounds of the main courtyard, acts of Puja (worship) take place throughout the day, either individually or communally. The temple and its community of monks is an important center for the Tibetan Buddhists of Nepal. BODHNATH STUPA—Also on the outskirts of the city, Bodhnath Stupa is one of the largest stupas in the world. It is an immense whitewashed structure which rises above the carefully tilled farms of the surrounding countryside. A number of stalls ring the stupa in which religious articles are sold.

Although there are many new buildings in Kathmandu, the city is essentially made up of older buildings of brick and ornately carved wood. The heart of the city is its Durbar Square, a complex of Hindu and Buddhist temples, open-air markets, and stalls. Villagers from outlying districts bring their produce and handicrafts here to sell and barter. Narrow and crowded alleys contain a rich variety of small stores, roadside shrines, roaming cows, extremely inexpensive hotels and restaurants, etc. Three miles southwest of Kathmandu is the city of Patan, considered to be the artistic capital of the nation. Nine miles to the east of Kathmandu is the city of Bhadgaon, a center of ancient art and architecture. Both cities are famous for their elaborately carved and decorated temples, paintings, bronzework, etc. The Tibetan Refugee Center in Patan is famous for the weaving and sale of Tibetan rugs.

Kathmandu, Nepal 70

Lumbini

The easiest access to Lumbini is by air from Kathmandu to the town of Bhairawa and from Bhairawa to Lumbini along a newly-completed road some 13 miles long. There is also a minibus which leaves Kathmandu at 6 AM and arrives at Bhairawa at 6 PM. Refer to the Tourist Office in Kathmandu. The third access to Lumbini is from the Indian side which is equally difficult. One can drive by bus or car from Lucknow or Gorakhpur, a full day's trip in either case.

Accomodations in Lumbini are minimal. There is a Government Resthouse with simply a room and a bed (no linen). The Tibetan Temple and the Theravada Mahabodhi Society temple also have pilgrim accomodations. Lumbini is a miniscule village and meals are limited to fruits and snacks at roadside stalls. If you stay in Lumbini, you will be roughing it, but for less than 50 cents a day. Better meals and accomodations are available in Bhairawa or Gorakhpur across the border in India.

Nothing remains of ancient Lumbini save the commemorative pillar erected by the Emperor Ashoka in 249 B.C. and scattered foundation stones of monasteries and temples. Despite this fact, and the scarcity of accomodations, pilgrims come in a steady stream to this birthplace of the Buddha.

On the request of the late United Nations Secretary-General U Thant in 1967, the Government of Nepal and the United Nations Development Program have embarked upon a Lumbini development program with the master plan designed by the renown Japanese architect Kenzo Tange. The newly completed road from Bhairawa to Lumbini is part of the development project.

INDIA
Patna

From Kathmandu the pilgrimage group flew to Patna, the capital of the state of Bihar. Patna was formerly the ancient city of Pataliputra which reached its zenith of glory under the reign of the Emperor Ashoka of the Maurya Empire in the 3rd century B.C. During this period, it was one of the great cities of the world. Nothing of its former magnificence remains today, however, except for a few polished pillars of what is believed to be the remains of a royal palace. Patna today is the administrative center for Bihar State and the starting point for the nearby Buddhist sites. It is also an important religious center for the Sikhas, being the birthplace of Guru Govind Singh the 10th and last Sikh Guru. Room and board in Patna ranges from $1.00 to $10.00 per day with a rather wide range of Indian and Western-style accomodations.

Nalanda

Approximately 60 miles southeast of Patna lie the sprawling remains of Nalanda University, one of the most renown seats of learning of the ancient world. As is the case with most of the Buddhist sites, there are no western-style accomodations. Nalanda today is a small village with no hotels or restaurants. Very simple rooms can be found at the Inspection Bungalow and the Nalanda Rest House for a few cents a day. The Pali Institute sometimes has rooms for free. Food is limited to snacks and fruit at roadside stalls. If you are ready for a reorientation in time and space, a few days in Nalanda is well worth the inconveniences. The

Aurangabad, India 71

ruins of Nalanda should be leisurely explored as well as the small museum nearby. From Patna, Nalanda can be reached by bus or cab. The Government of India Tourist Office in Patna will arrange for cabs or you can bargain with the individual cab driver yourself. The cab fare, however, is based on a round trip from Patna to Nalanda, Rajgir and back. There is an additional charge for an overnight stay. Far more time consuming but very much cheaper is the regular bus service from Patna to Nalanda.

Rajgir

Rajgir lies some 7 miles south of Nalanda. It can be reached by regular bus service which stops at Nalanda on its way to Rajgir from Bihar Sharif. Rajgir is an important religious center for Jains as well as for Buddhists and a number of Indian-style hotels are available. All of these however are simple rooms with beds, some dormitory style, and shared bathing facilities. Basic but comfortable is the Tourist Bungalow for about 40 cents per person per day with no meals. Dormitory rooms are even cheaper. In Rajgir, signs reading "hotel" mean restaurant. Many of these "hotels" surround the open space in front of the hot springs. A fairly filling meal for a few cents can be obtained at these "hotels." For restaurants with menus, try the south Indian on the grounds of the Burmese Temple and restaurants in the new town part of Rajgir.

Bodhgaya

Bodhgaya is approximately 50 miles southwest of Rajgir. There is a regular bus service from Rajgir to Bodhgaya via Gaya.

The trip will take between 6 to 10 hours depending on how many stops the bus makes at the many villages along the road. It will also make a half hour to one hour stop at Gaya, a large city sacred to the god Vishnu and the second most sacred city in India next to Varanasi for the Hindus. It is the center for Vishnu worship on behalf of one's ancestors, drawing Hindu pilgrims to the Vishnupada Temple which is said to enshrine the footprints of the Lord Vishnu. Eight miles to the south of Gaya is the quiet village of Bodhgaya. It is the center of the Buddhist world and the site most frequented by Buddhist pilgrims.

Again there are no western-style hotels. In recent years a number of pilgrim guest houses have been built to accomodate visitors. The best accomodations are at the Traveller's Lodge and the Rest House of the Japanese Temple, both of which have comfortable private rooms with bath. These rooms run from $2.00 to $3.00 per day per person. Cheaper accomodations can be had at the Birla Rest House—extremely simple rooms with shared bath. Bunk space is available in the tent restaurants next to the Tibetan Temple and free sleeping quarters are available at the Mahabodhi Rest House. Several temples provide sleeping quarters without charge. A small donation however, is not only proper but greatly appreciated.

There are no western-style restaurants but an abundance of fruit and snack stalls. Small Indian restaurants are numerous. Inexpensive and filling are the tent restaurants of the Tibetans next to the Tibetan Temple. Also in the village southwest of the Mahabodhi Temple, there is an outdoor restaurant run by a gentle Tibetan woman who will serve you a hearty Tibetan meal for a few cents.

The major temples and sites in Bodhgaya are all within walking distance or can easily be reached by Tanka (horse carts) for a few cents.

Varanasi (Benares)

To reach Varanasi you must take the train from Gaya Station. There is an early morning bus from Bodhgaya to Gaya. In Varanasi there are several luxury hotels such as the Clarks, Varnasi, Hotel de Paris, etc. ranging in cost from $10.00 to $20.00 per person per day. If you want to splurge, Varanasi is one city where you can do so. Otherwise simple but comfortable accomodations can be found at the Uttar Pradesh Government Tourist Bungalow on Parade Kothi Road, the Tourist Dak Bungalow next to the Hotel de Paris, and the Tourist Lodge in the Mall. These range from about $2.00 to $6.00 per double room with bath.

In Varanasi, a wide selection of food is available at a wide range of prices. For a living tourist attraction among student travelers, visit Simon at his Chinese restaurant across the street from the Uttar Pradesh Government Tourist Bungalow—an experience.

Varanasi is older than recorded time and the center of the Hindu world. Its several thousand temples are dedicated to the worship of the God Shiva. This microcosm of the Hindu world plays out its role on the banks of the sacred River Ganges. Its endless narrow and twisting streets will more than amply reward the curious explorer. For tourist information, visit the Government Tourist Office on the Mall.

Sarnath

Six miles north of Varanasi is Sarnath, the site of the Buddha's first sermon.

Delhi, India 72

Bombay, India 73

The Government Tourist Bungalow in Sarnath provides comfortable accomodations in a quiet and relaxed setting. Don't miss the museum at Sarnath for some of the finest examples of Indian Buddhist art.

Khajuraho

Khajuraho today is a sleepy little village. In the 10th and 11th centuries however, it was an important center of Hindu culture. Twenty temples remain from this period. These Hindu and Jain temples are covered with sculpture celebrating life and its pleasures. The amorous scenes of handsome men and voluptuous women in various positions of love are famous the world over.

Khajuraho is an hour's flight from Varanasi. The flight leaves daily from Varanasi and proceeds to Agra and New Delhi. One can stay overnight in Khajuraho and catch the next flight to Agra the following morning. Khajuraho can also be reached by train and bus via Allahabad and Satna.

The Khajuraho Tourist Bungalow offers Spartan accomodations for about 75 cents per person per night. Simple rope-beds in small rooms with shared cold water bath. On our visit, the amiable cook was from Kerala and prepared tasty meals for about 15 cents to 25 cents. Khajuraho is a slow moving town and is a relaxing change from the large cities. An overnight stay will give you ample time to explore the temples, all of them within walking distance.

Agra

Agra of course is the city of the Taj Mahal. Just to view this marvel of white marble would be worth the trip. In and around Agra however, are other examples of the splendor of Mughal India. Sikandra, Agra Fort, Itmad-Ud-Daulah Mausoleum, Fatepur Sikri, and many other examples of Mughal architecture and stonework attest to the brilliance of Mughal civilization. The nearby city of Mathura is important to two religious traditions. Mathura is said to be the birthplace of Krishna, the eighth incarnation of the god Vishnu. It was also one of the great centers of Buddhist sculpture. The Mathura style of sculpture which began in the 1st century A.D. has had great influence on all subsequent Indian art. There is an excellent government museum in Mathura containing masterworks of the Mathura style.

Comfortable hotels such as the Grand Hotel have large rooms with hot showers and western-style toilets for $5.00 to $6.00 per person per double.

Sanchi

It will take a full day by train to get to Sanchi from Agra (90 rupees). You must request the stationmaster at Agra to have the train stop at Sanchi. The train leaves Agra in the morning and arrives at Sanchi late that night. Accomodations are limited in Sanchi and food is of the snack and food stall type. Best accomodations are at the Travellers' Lodge which has a restaurant. The Mahabodhi Society has a pilgrim's rest house immediately in front of the railway station. They have simple rooms with shared baths. There is no charge but a donation to help continue the good work of the society will be appreciated. The Buddhist monks there are most hospitable. The Great Stupa of Sanchi is situated on a hill overlooking the village.

Ajanta

To get to the cave temples of Ajanta and Ellora from Sanchi, you must take the train from Sanchi to the city of Jalgaon (22 rupees). The train leaves Sanchi in the afternoon and arrives late in the evening at Jalgaon. There is then a layover of 6 or 7 hours until the bus runs to to Ajanta and Aurangabad begin in the morning.

There are railway retiring rooms at the station in Jalgaon. The bus station is about a mile away from the railway station. With some determined bargaining, you can get a Tanka (horse cart) ride for a few cents. The distance to Ajanta is 37 miles and takes about one hour (3 rupees). Accomodations at Ajanta are very limited and it is best to stay in Aurangabad some 66 miles beyond Ajanta (5 rupees). Snacks and light meals are available at Ajanta. Busses stop regularly throughout the day at Ajanta, enabling you to spend a full day at Ajanta and its incredible cave temples.

Aurangabad

Aurangabad is a rather sprawling Muslim town famous primarily for its close proximity to Ajanta and Ellora. There are several western-style hotels and many excellent Indian style hotels. The family-run Printravel Hotel has comfortable rooms (doubles and triples) with hot showers, western toilets and full board (breakfast and dinner) for about $5.00 per person per day. The food is excellent. It is very near the Indian Airlines office and the Government Tourist Office. Busses leave regularly for Ajanta and Ellora. There are also special bus tours of both sites as well as Daulatabad Fort and other sites in the city. Ellora is 18 miles from Aurangabad. From Aurangabad, one can get to Bombay by plane, bus or train. The train is the cheapest but involves a transfer at Manmad. Luxury busses are available at a higher cost but these too will take

Ajanta, India 74

" My disciples, the last moment has come.
But do not forget that death is but the vanishing of a body.
The body was born,
so sickness and death is unavoidable.
But the true Buddha is not a human body: —
it is Enlightenment."

— The Buddha —

Ajanta, India 75

a full day to get to Bombay. There are daily flights from Aurangabad to Bombay which take about an hour and at very reasonable prices.

Bombay

Bombay is perhaps the most modern and most cosmopolitan city in India. Room and board ranges from primitive to princely with corresponding prices. The area of Santa Cruz near the International Airport is generally cheaper than in Bombay itself. Train fare from Santa Cruz to downtown Bombay is about 10 cents with trains running on a regular and frequent schedule. Indian-style hotels with shower run around $3.00 or $4.00 per person per double in the Santa Cruz area. Bombay is the place to indulge your appetite, especially seafood. A short distance from Bombay are the Buddhist cave temples of Kanheri and Karla.

Madra

The pilgrimage group flew from Bombay to Madras to save time. The inexpensive train ride from Bombay to Madras takes 2½ days. South India is almost another country. There are important differences politically, racially, linguistically, and culturally. South India is also the stronghold of Hindu orthodoxy. Buddhism was said to have even penetrated into the south of India and important ruins are still to be found at Amaravati and Nagarjunikonda in the state of Andhra Pradesh. Madras is the largest city in south India. The weather is warm to hot throughout the year. Prices are generally lower in the south than in the north. A very comfortable double room with hot showers, air conditioning, western toilets, and restaurant such as found at the Geetha Hotel will run about $3.00 per person. Generally hot but very good vegetarian meals are a specialty of cooking in the south.

Side trips to the seaside temples of Mahabalipuram and the temple town of Kanchipuram are musts. They are easily reached by public bus. Hindu temples of enormous size abound in Kanchipuram.

Tiruchirapalli

Tiruchirapalli or Trichy is a day's train ride south of Madras. Indian-style hotels such as the Hotel Aristo offer moderated size doubles with shower, western toilet, and air conditioning for about $2.00 to $3.00 per person. Within easy travel by bus or train from Trichy are the famous Hindu temples of Srirangam, Thanjavur, and Madurai. Literally temple towns with colossal gateways soaring up to 200 feet in the air, the temples of this region represent the best examples of south Indian architecture.

From Trichy one can fly to Colombo, the capital of Sri Lanka. If you are not pressed for time, take the train from Madurai to Rameswaram with its magnificent temple dedicated to the god Rama. From Rameswaram there is a ferryboat which crosses over to Sri Lanka twice a week except for the month of December. The ferry lands at Talaimannar in Sri Lanka. There is a train connecting Talaimannar with the cities of Anuradhapura and Colombo. This is the most inexpensive route and by far the most interesting, but also the most time consuming.

SRI LANKA (formerly CEYLON)

The majority of the people of Sri Lanka are Buddhists of the Theravada school. Buddhism in Sri Lanka is a living tradition and its influence on daily life is great indeed. The ancient cities of Anuradhapura, Polonnaruwa, Sigiriya, and Dambulla developed under the influence of Buddhist culture and vast man-made lakes, parks, shrines, temples, stupas and monasteries are to be found in these ancient cities. The present-day centers of Buddhist activity and culture are to be found in the cities of Kandy and Colombo.

Prices for room and board are higher than in India, approximately $2.00 more than for comparable accomodations and food in India.

Anuradhapura

Anuradhapura was founded in the 5th century B.C. and became the first great Buddhist capital of Sri Lanka. The remains of the sacred city are scattered over an enormous area containing numerous shrines, monasteries, temples, stupas, etc. in various stages of excavation. The stupendous Ruwanwelisaya, one of the largest stupas in the world, towers over the lush countryside. Many of the ancient monuments are still in use and the sacred area forbids any means of transportation other than by foot. The most treasured object in the ancient city is the sacred Bo Tree. This is a tree descended from a slip taken from the original tree under which Siddhartha became the Buddha. It was brought to Sri Lanka by the daugher of the Emperor Ashoka. It is thus the oldest historically documented tree in the world and the object of great veneration by Buddhists. Eight miles east of Anuradhapura is Mihintale, a mountain atop which are a number of monasteries. This is the spot where Prince Mahinda, son of the Emperor Ashoka, brought Buddhism to Sri Lanka in 247 B.C.

Rambling hotels from the British period are found within the ancient city. The Tissawewa Hotel has showers, western toilets, large dining and lounging rooms, and spacious grounds. Doubles run from $4.00 to $7.00 for room only. With two delicious meals included, the cost is between $12.00 and $16.00 per double. Cheaper accomodations can be found in the new town area in the $1.00 to $5.00 range.

Polonnaruwa-Sigiriya-Dambulla

To reach Polonnaruwa and Sigiriya from Anuradhapura, one must take a bus or car. Polonnaruwa was the second great capital city of the ancient Buddhist kings. An elaborate irrigation system of man-made lakes and aqueducts worked out in an intricate grid pattern can still be seen. Remains of the king's palace, various religious edifices and the famous Buddha images of the Gal Vihare are to be found in Polonnaruwa. Polonnaruwa is a tourist center and prices are generally higher than in Anuradhapura.

The trip from Polonnaruwa to Kandy must also be taken by bus or car. This route will take you past the towns of Sigiriya and Dambulla. Sigiriya is a city built high atop a rock outcropping. In caves in the side of the rock outcropping are some lovely fresco paintings.

In Dambulla are also found cave temples with some very ancient fresco paintings as well as a recumbent Buddha carved from solid rock some 45 feet long.

Kandy

Kandy was the capital of the last Sri Lanka kingdom. It resisted the British until 1815. It is nestled in the highlands of the island with the city surrounding a large man-made lake. Today it is a center of Buddhist culture and scholarship. The most important building in Kandy is the Dalada Maligawa or the Temple of the Tooth which houses a tooth relic of the Buddha. In July/August of each year, the sacred tooth relic is brought out of the temple on the back of an elephant accompanied by a procession of Kandyan chieftains, drummers, dancers, attendants, dignitaries, etc. This festival called the Esala Perahera builds up to a climax over a period of ten days into what is without a doubt the most spectacular festival in Asia. Nearby Kandy is the Royal Botanic Gardens, one of the best tropical gardens in the world. Also nearby is the University of Ceylon. Kandy is also the headquarters of the Buddhist Publication Society with a large library of Buddhist literature in English. The Society is also very helpful in giving information to those interested in Buddhist meditation and study.

The Queens Hotel in Kandy is an old but comfortable hotel on the edge of the lake. Double rooms with shared bath run about $5.00 per person. This includes a hearty English breakfast. Much cheaper, sometimes free accomodations are at the YMCA. The best food is in the small restaurants in the town. Be careful, Sri Lanka curry can be explosively hot.

Colombo

From Kandy you ride the train down to the coast through countryside so beautiful and so bright green it hurts your eyes. In Colombo you can have accomodations ranging from Buddhist and Christian youth centers to luxury hotels. The temples of Kelaniya and Gangaramaya in Colombo provide a good introduction to Buddhism in Sri Lanka.

May the Hidden Splendor within us all
be close to its unfolding
May the lotus not be impeded in
its flowering.

Ajanta, India 76

Photographic Index

Photographed by Dean-Koga. All other photographs by Alan Ohashi.

Selected photographs are available upon request.
Please indicate photograph number, photographer name
and short description of photo.
Address inquiries to :

Alan Ohashi
c/o 1336 W. 36th Place
 Los Angeles, California   U.S.A
or:
Heian International Publishing Company
c/o T. Yukawa
 P.O. Box 2402
 South San Francisco, California U.S.A

We would like to acknowledge
the following for their help in making
this book a reality...........

Kinnara
Senshin Buddhist Temple
Visual Communications/Asian American Studies Central
Tetsuya Yukawa
Glen Akira Iwasaki
Russell Hamada
Claudia Moriguchi
Ed Ikuta
Buddhist Churches of America
Shirley Kodani
Steve Tatsukawa
Alan Kondo

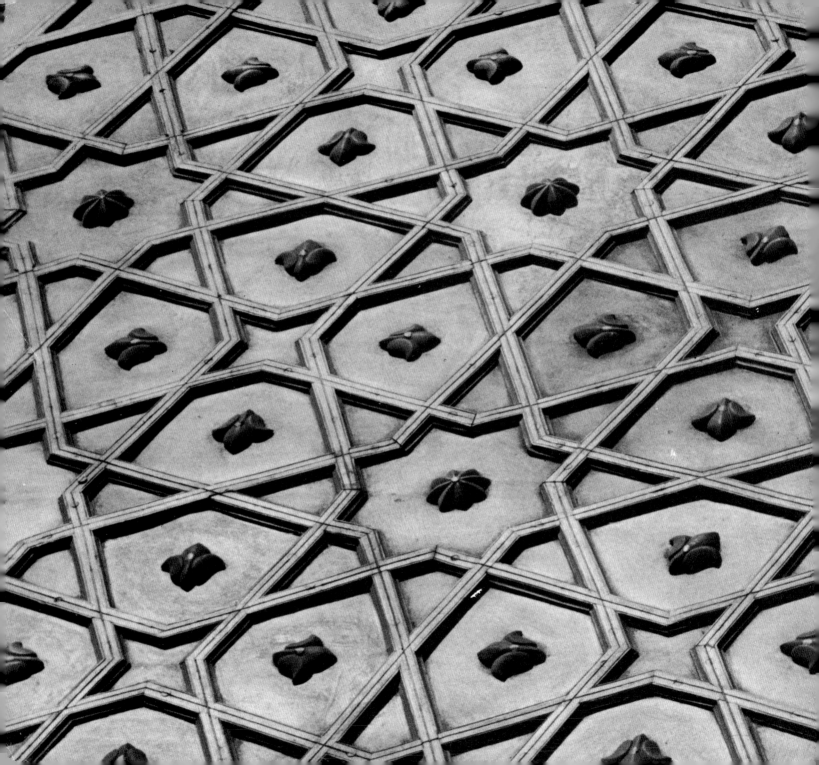